I am me.
You are you.
I am special.
You are too!

I am special because
I am me!

It's not because of the color of
my hair or the color of my eyes.
It's not because the color of my
skin or because of my size.

It's not because of what I have
or because of where I live.
It's not because of where I'm
going or because of where
I've been.

It's not because of what I wear or who my family is.
It's not because I'm healthy, nor because I'm sick.

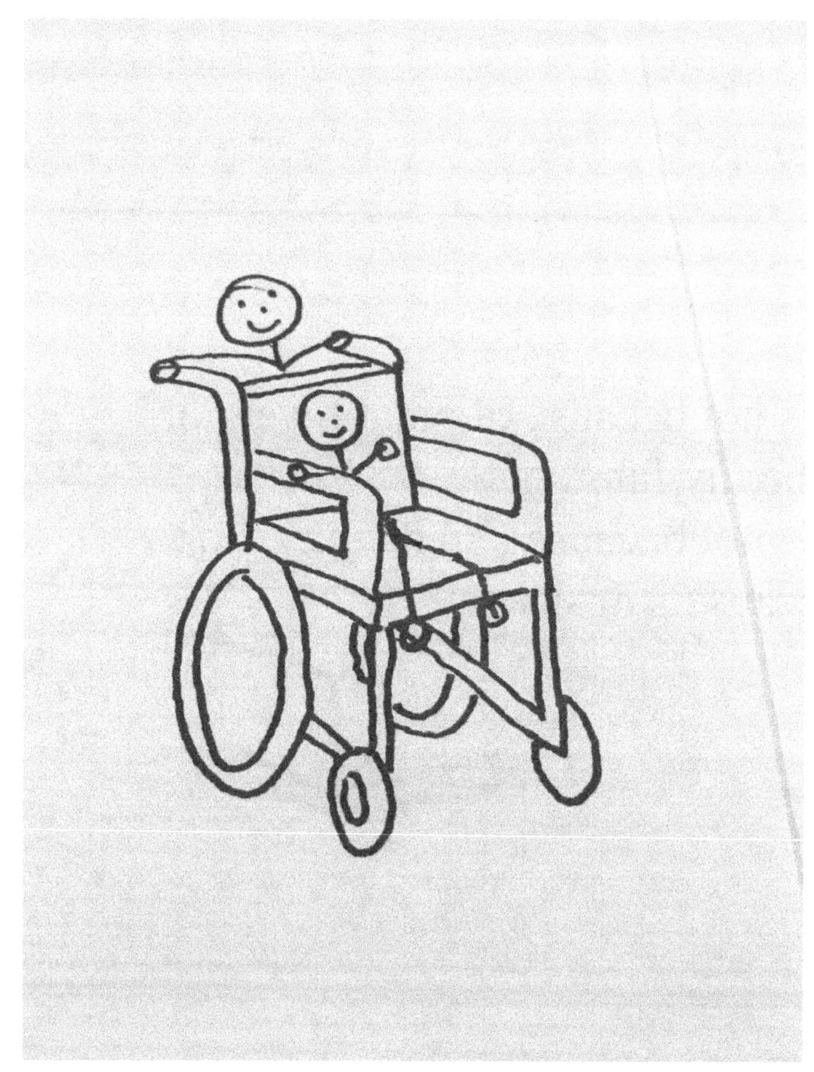

It's not because I need help
or because I'm really smart.
It's not because I have two
hands or because my legs
don't work.

Hooray

It's not because I play ball
or because I cheer.

It's not because I wear glasses or because I can hear. It's not because I am brave or because I sometimes fear.

Fa La La

It's not because of how I talk, with
my hands or with my mouth. It's not
because I can sing or because I can
only shout.

It's not because I am fast.
It's not because I'm slow.
It's not because I have two
homes and I'm always on
the go.

I am special because of
what is in my heart.
What fills our hearts is what
makes us who we are.
That is what makes
us special.

Love

In giving or receiving,
a heart full of LOVE
is the most special gift
by far.

Love has no boundaries.

I am special!
You are special!

Dedicated
To
Everyone!

www.ingramcontent.com/pod-product-compliance
Lightning Source LLC
Chambersburg PA
CBHW051410150726
48000CB00003B/1406